My
Favorite
Dogs

# ROTTWEILER

## Jinny Johnson

A⁺

**Smart Apple Media**

Published by Smart Apple Media,
an imprint of Black Rabbit Books
P.O. Box 3263, Mankato, Minnesota, 56002
www.blackrabbitbooks.com

Designed by Hel James
Edited by Mary-Jane Wilkins

Library of Congress Cataloging-in-Publication Data
Johnson, Jinny
  Rottweiler / Jinny Johnson.
    pages cm. -- (My favorite dogs)
  Summary: "Describes the characteristics of the Rottweiler
and how to care for it"-- Provided by publisher.
  Audience: Grades K to 3.
  Includes index.
  ISBN 978-1-62588-178-6
  1. Rottweiler dog--Juvenile literature.  I. Title.
  SF429.R7D53 2015
  636.73--dc23
                       2014003961

Photo acknowledgements
t = top, b = bottom
title page f8grapher; 3 cynoclub; 4 Ersler Dmitry; 5 Lee319; 6 Rita
Kochmarjova/all Shutterstock; 7 ???iana Makotra/Thinkstock; 8 Margo
Harrison; 10 Degtyaryov Andrey/both Shutterstock; 11 cynoclub/
Thinkstock; 12t Liliya Kulianionak, b Stephen Coburn; 13t NKLRDVC/
all Shutterstock, b cynoclub/Thinkstock; 14 tony4urban; 15t cynoclub,
b Rita Kochmarjova; 16 Milan Vachal/all Shutterstock; 17 © Peer Körner/
dpa/Corbis; 18 Ersler Dmitry; 19 hempuli/Shutterstock; 20 egonzitter;
21 TATYANA MAKOTRA; 22 UroshPetrovic/all Thinkstock;
23 Jagodka/Shutterstock
Cover cynoclub/Shutterstock

Printed in China

DAD0053
032014
9 8 7 6 5 4 3 2 1

# Contents

# I'm a Rottweiler!

I know I look tough,
but you'd be surprised—
I can be a gentle, loyal,
loving companion.

Train me well and I will
be your perfect family pet.

# What I Need

I like to be busy, so please take me out for lots of exercise. I'm happy living in an apartment as long as I can go out and run around often.

I love my family, but I watch out for strangers and I'm a good guard dog. I always do my best to protect my people.

# The Rottweiler

Tail sometimes docked

Coarse, straight coat

Color:
Black with
tan markings

Height:
Male
24-27 inches
(61-68.5 cm);
female
22-25 inches
(56-63.5 cm)

Weight:
55-70 pounds
(25-32 kg)

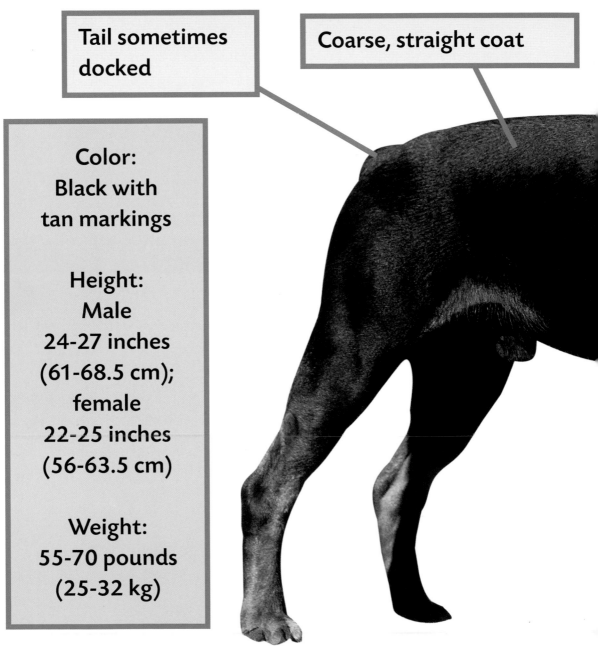

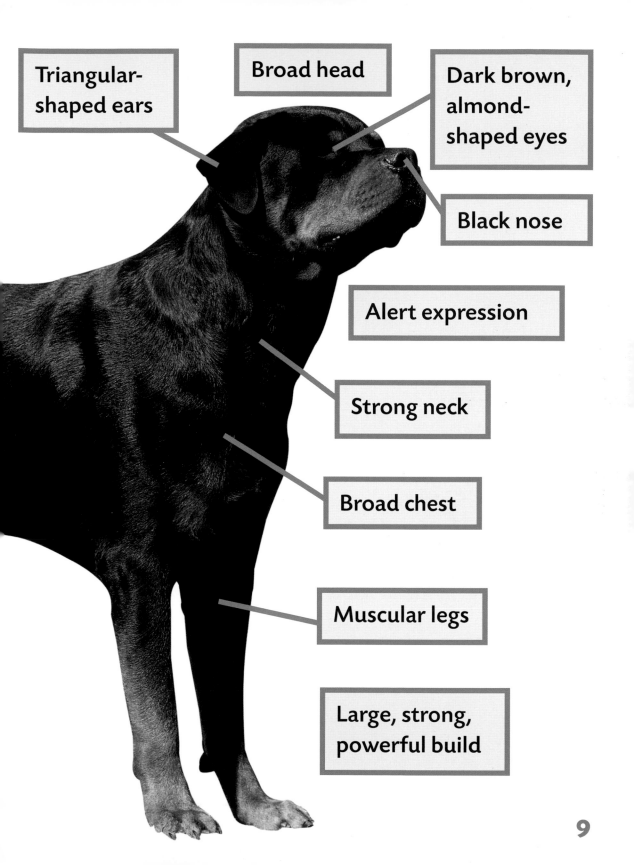

Triangular-shaped ears

Broad head

Dark brown, almond-shaped eyes

Black nose

Alert expression

Strong neck

Broad chest

Muscular legs

Large, strong, powerful build

# All About Rottweilers

Rottweilers were first bred in Germany. They are probably descended from dogs used in ancient Rome as herders and guard dogs.

These dogs also pulled carts filled with logs.

Rottweilers are hard workers and love to have a job to do.

Rottweilers enjoy agility trials, too.

# Growing Up

Rottweiler pups are very cute and their big brown eyes will melt your heart. Your pup needs to be with his mom until he is eight weeks old,

then he will be ready
for his new home.

Be very gentle while
he settles in and
gets to know you.

In no time
your little pup
will grow into a
big, strong dog.

# Training Your Rottweiler

Rottweilers are powerful dogs and need careful training. A rottie must understand that you are in charge and that he must obey. Start training when your dog is young and small.

A properly trained Rottweiler is a great family dog and good with children. But an untrained Rottweiler is hard to control and could be dangerous.

Rottweilers love to run and they enjoy chasing a ball.

# Working Dogs

A Rottweiler's bravery, strength, and protective instinct make him a great guard dog. He is fearless when defending those he loves.

Rottweilers are very intelligent and are used for police work. Their calm confidence also makes them good service dogs, helping people with disabilities.

# Therapy Dog

Therapy dogs are specially trained to visit people in hospitals to cheer them up.

A Rottweiler's gentle nature makes it a good therapy dog. These dogs love people and they like to be petted.

# Your Healthy Rottweiler

Make sure you buy your pup from a good breeder. Rottweilers can have hip problems.

Brush his short coat every week to keep your dog looking good, and bathe him when necessary.

Rottweilers can be greedy and put on weight. Don't feed him too many treats.

# Caring for Your Rottweiler

You and your family must think carefully before buying a Rottweiler. He may look cute as a puppy, but he will become a large dog and he may live for 10-12 years.

Every day your dog must have food, water, and exercise, as well as lots of love and care. He will also need

to go to the vet for regular checks and vaccinations. When you and your family go out or away, you will have to make plans for your dog to be looked after.

# Useful Words

**breed**
A particular type of dog.

**service dog**
A dog that is trained to help disabled people with everyday tasks.

**vaccinations**
Injections given by the vet to protect your dog against certain illnesses.

# Index